MW01027746

LEARNING THE LOGIC OF SUBCHAPTER K:
PROBLEMS AND ASSIGNMENTS FOR A COURSE IN THE TAXATION OF PARTNERSHIPS

By

Laura E. Cunningham
Professor of Law
Benjamin N. Cardozo School of Law

Noël B. Cunningham
Professor of Law
New York University School of Law

AMERICAN CASEBOOK SERIES®

THOMSON
™
WEST

Mat #40769334

American Casebook Series and West Group are trademarks
registered in the U.S. Patent and Trademark Office.

© 2008 Thomson/West
      610 Opperman Drive
      St. Paul, MN 55123
      1–800–313–9378

Printed in the United States of America

ISBN: 978–0–314–19894–5

TEXT IS PRINTED ON 10% POST
CONSUMER RECYCLED PAPER

Preface and Acknowledgement

The contents of this book provide the basis for a J.D. or graduate level course in the taxation of partnerships. They are designed to be used in conjunction with Cunningham & Cunningham, *The Logic of Subchapter K: A Conceptual Guide to the Taxation of Partnerships*, West Publishing (3rd Edition), and all assignments to **Logic** refer to that text. Essential to the course is a thorough reading of the assigned Code and Regulations sections as well. The latter assignments are intended to be cumulative: each chapter builds on materials learned in earlier chapters.

These problems were developed over our eighteen years of teaching Partnership Taxation at New York University School of Law and the Benjamin N. Cardozo School of Law. Many colleagues and students have had a hand in their development. Nevertheless, our friend and colleague Len Schmolka is deserving of special mention. Because of his invaluable help in drafting the problems and the answers as well, we dedicate this book to him. Thanks Len!

We, of course, accept full responsibility for all errors.

Noël B. Cunningham
Laura E. Cunningham
July, 2008

Table of Contents

Preface & Acknowledgement i

Chapter One: Choice of Entity 1

Chapter Two: Partnership Formation 2

Chapter Three: Partnership Operations 5

Chapter Four: Capital Accounts 7

Chapter Five: Substantial Economic Effect 10

Chapter Six: Allocation of Nonrecourse Deductions 14

Chapter Seven: Contributions of Property 16

Chapter Eight: Partnership Liabilities 19

Chapter Nine: Partner/Partnership Transactions 22

Chapter Ten: Sales of Partnership Interests 25

Chapter Eleven: Distributions: the Basics 28

Chapter Twelve: Optional Basis Adjustment 31

Chapter Thirteen: Disproportionate Distributions 34

Chapter Fourteen: Retirement and Death of Partners 37

Chapter Fifteen: Disguised Sales and Exchanges 41

Chapter One
Choice of Entity

Assignment:

Logic: Chapter One

Code: §§ 701, 761(a), 7701(a)(2) & (3). Skim §§ 702, 703(b), 706 (a) and 7704.

Regulations: §§ 1.761-1(a)-(c), -2(a), §§ 301.7701-1(a), -2(a) & (b), and -3(a) & (b)(1)
and -4(a) & (b).

Recommended Reading: Commission v. Culbertson, 337 U.S. 733 (1949)

1.   *A* and *B* purchase unimproved land as cotenants. In each of the following
alternatives, determine whether *A* and *B* have created an "entity" for tax purposes:

a. They hold the land for appreciation;

b. They lease the land to *Z* who uses the land for farming;

c. They construct a motel on the land and hire *C* to manage the motel for
them.

2.   *A, B* and *C* have decided to leave their current positions as software designers in a
large company and to start up their own firm. *A* and *B* have been very successful and are
now quite wealthy. *C*, on the other hand, is a brilliant young programmer who is still
paying off student loans. Although *A* and *B* both plan to invest capital in the new firm,
they hope to attract additional outside investors. They have come to you for advice in
setting up their new venture. What would you suggest?

Assignment:

Logic: Chapter Two and skim pages 31-40 of Chapter Four

Code & Regulations:

> **Problem 1:** Code §§ 704(c)(1)(A), 721, 722, 723, 724, 1223(1) & (2), 1245(b)(3), 7701(a)(42) - (45); Regs. §§ 1.721-1(a), 1.722-1, 1.723-1 , 1223-3(b)(1).

> **Problem 2:** Code §§ 704(c)(3), 731(a), (b), (c)(1), 733, 752(a) & (b); Reg. §§ 1.752-1(a) - (f), 1.752-2(a).

Recommended Reading: *Stafford v. United States*, 611 F.2d 990 (5th Cir. 1980); *Oden v. Commissioner,* 410 TCM 1285 (1981).

Problems:

1. A, B and C, three individuals, form a general partnership by contributing the following property in exchange for equal undivided 1/3 interests in the partnership:

> A contributes Land, a capital asset A acquired several years ago, worth $100 in which A has a tax basis of $40.

> B contributes machinery with a basis of $25 and a value of $60, plus $40 in cash. B purchased the machinery several years ago for $75 and has taken $50 of depreciation.

> C contributes stock with a value of $100 in which C has a basis of $160. C purchased the stock 3 years ago as an investment

(a) What gain and/or loss will be recognized by the partners and the partnership on formation?

(b) What will be the partnership's "inside basis" and holding period for the contributed assets?

(c) What will be the partners' "outside bases" and holding period for their partnership interests?

(d) Construct an opening balance sheet for ABC. Your balance sheet should be in the following form:

Assets			Liabilities & Capital		
	Basis	*Book*	*Liabilities*		
Cash	$	$			
Other assets					
			Capital Accounts		
				Tax	*Book*
			A	$	$
			B		
			C		

2. D, E and F form a partnership by contributing the various assets described below (in each case worth $200 net of liabilities) in exchange for equal 1/3 interests in the partnership's capital, profits and losses. The partnership assumes all liabilities encumbering the contributed assets.

   D contributes land with a fair market value of $400, which is encumbered by a recourse mortgage of $240. D's has held the land for several years as an investment, and his basis in the land is $100. D also contributes $40 in cash.

   E contributes a building, a § 1231 asset, with a value of $260 in which E has an adjusted basis of $130. The building was purchased several years ago by E and is subject to a recourse mortgage $60.

   F, a cash method taxpayer, contributes zero basis accounts receivable from his business worth $350, and assigns his accounts payable of $150 to the partnership.

NOTE: For purposes of this problem, ignore the possibility that there might be a disguised sale, assume that DEF uses the traditional method for making § 704(c) allocations, and finally assume that the partnership will allocate the liabilities it assumes equally among the partners.

(a) With respect to each partner,

   (i) Is any gain or loss recognized?

   (ii) What is her outside basis?

(b) With respect to DEF:

    (1) Does it recognize any gain or loss on formation?

    (2) What is its inside basis in the contributed property?

(c) Construct an opening balance sheet for the partnership similar to the one you constructed in Problem 1(d), above.

(d) How would the consequences to D differ, if, instead of contributing the $40 of cash, D contributed her own negotiable promissory note for $40, bearing adequate stated interest?

Chapter Three
Partnership Operations

Part A. Taxable Years and Methods of Accounting

Assignment:

Logic: pages 21-26

Code: §§ 448(a) – (c), 706(a) & (b). Skim §§ 444, 7519.

Regulations: §§ 1.706-1(a), (b)(1)-(3).

Problems:

1. A, B, and C Corp. form a partnership. A and B are individual, cash method, calendar year taxpayers. C Corp. is a small corporation that, over the last three years, has had average annual gross receipts in excess of $6 million. C Corp. is an accrual method taxpayer using a June 30 fiscal year. The partners share profits, losses and capital equally.

    a. The ABC partnership must choose a taxable year. If there were no constraints on this choice, what taxable year would you expect A to favor? C Corp.?

    b. What is ABC's "required taxable year" within the meaning of § 444(e)?

    c. ABC must also choose a method of accounting. Is it permitted to elect to use the cash method of accounting?

2. X, Y and Z form a partnership. X is a corporation with a 7/31 fiscal year, Y is a corporation with a 1/31 fiscal year, and Z is a calendar year individual. What is the partnership's required taxable year if the partners share profits and capital in the following alternative proportions:

    a. 60% X, 20% Y, 20% Z

    b. 50% X, 30% Y, 20% Z

    c. Assume the XYZ partnership's principal business activity is the preparation of tax returns. What taxable year might it prefer? Is that choice available to it?

Part B. The Basics of Taxing Partnership Operations

Assignment:

Logic: pages 26-30

Code: §§ 701, 702, 703, 704(a), 705(a), 706(a), 724. Skim § 6031.

Regulations: §§ 1.702-1(a)(8), (b), 1.705-1(a), 1.706-1(a).

Problem:

The AB partnership had the following income and expenses for the past calendar year:

(1) Gross income from business operations	$130
(2) Expenses deductible under § 162(a)	40
(3) Depreciation on machinery (calculated under the 200% declining balance method)	30
(4) Charitable gifts	20
(5) Gain on sale of equipment used in the partnership business, $20 of which is ordinary under § 1245(a), and $10 of which is §1231 gain	30
(6) Short-term capital gain on stock sale	10
(7) Interest on tax exempt bonds	40
(8) Dividends on stock	20
(9) Gain on the sale of land held for 4 years by the partnership for investment purposes	100

A and B are equal partners who use the calendar year as their taxable years.

1. How will the partnership, A and B report these items?

2. Would the treatment of the gain in item (9) be different if A were a dealer in real estate? Assume, in the alternative, that the partnership acquired the land (i) from A as a contribution to the partnership, or (ii) by purchase from a third party.

3. A's adjusted basis for his partnership interest was $20 at the beginning of this taxable year of the partnership. What was his adjusted basis at the end of the year if the partnership made no distributions to the partners during the year?

4. How would your answer in 3 differ if on March 1 the partnership distributes $40 to each of the partners? See Reg. § 1.731-1(a)(1)(ii).

Chapter Four
Capital Accounts

Assignment:

Logic: ***Review carefully*** Chapter Four

Code: §§ 704(b), (c)(1)(A), 721(a), 722, 723, 752(a) & (b).

Regulations: §§ 1.704-1(b)(2)(iv)(a)-(i); 1.704-1(b)(4)(i).

Problem 1:

Basic Facts: *A* and *B* are partners in a newly-formed general partnership. They will share profits and losses equally (although their capital accounts may not always be equal). The partnership will maintain capital accounts in accordance with Regulation § 1.704-1(b)(2)(iv). The partners share recourse liabilities equally.

Prepare an opening balance sheet for the partnership (including tax capital accounts), reflecting the formation transaction described in part A below, and then determine the appropriate adjustments to the partners' capital accounts for each of the operating transactions described in part B below. While determining each of these adjustments for book purposes, keep in mind the effect, if any, of each of these transactions on *A's* and *B's* bases in their partnership interests.

A. Formation Transaction.

A contributes to the partnership:

	Basis	FMV
cash	$50	$50
land (encumbered by a $100 recourse mortgage that the partnership assumes)	100	200

B contributes to the partnership

	Basis	FMV
B's own note for $50 payable in 5 years bearing interest at the AFR	0	50
Cant make a note to yourself		
X's note payable to B	50	50
equipment	200	100

7

B. **Operating Transactions:**

1. The partnership earns $600 of ordinary income under § 702(a)(8).

2. The partnership receives $100 of bond interest that is tax exempt under §103

3. The partnership recognizes a $40 capital loss. Assume that A's current deduction for the loss is disallowed by § 1211, whereas B's share of the loss is currently deductible by him in full.

4. The partnership incurs $20 of nondeductible and noncapitalized expenditures described in § 705(a)(2)(B) (e.g., "key man" term life insurance policies on the lives of partners, of which the partnership is the owner and beneficiary).

5. The partnership borrows $100 from a bank.

6. Subsequently, A assumes full liability for the $100 bank debt in #5 above, and the bank releases the partnership from liability for the amount.

7. The partnership pays off the $100 bank debt previously assumed by A in #6.

8. The partnership pays off the mortgage encumbering the land contributed by A.

9. The partnership purchases common stock for $50. During the year the stock appreciates to $100, and the partnership distributes it to A.
   └ revaluation

10. The partnership purchases land for $200 by paying $100 cash and giving the seller a $100 recourse purchase-money mortgage. While the land is still worth $200, the partnership distributes it to A, who assumes the mortgage. Would it make any difference if A instead took the land subject to the mortgage (not becoming personally liable) and the partnership (and A and B as general partners) remained personally liable for its payment?

11. The partnership distributes to B its promissory note payable to B in a later year ($100 face amount with interest at the applicable federal rate).

Problem 2: Revaluations

The XYZ partnership has been operating for several years. All of its assets were purchased by the partnership, and at the end of the current year it's balance sheet, which has been expanded to show the current fair market value of assets and capital, is as follows:

Assets			Liabilities & Capital
	AB/Book	FMV	Liabilities
Cash	$600	$600	None
Accts. Rec.	0	200	
Equipment	100	200	
Stock	500	1000	
Land	300	1000	
Total	$1500	$3000	

	Capital Accounts	
	Tax/Book	FMV
X	$500	$1000
Y	500	1000
Z	500	1000
	$1500	$3000

On the last day of the current year, W joins the partnership. In exchange for a contribution of $1000 cash, he receives a 25% interest in partnership profits, losses, and capital.

1. Reconstruct the balance sheet of the partnership following W's admission to the partnership, assuming, in the alternative:

   a. The partnership does not elect to revalue it's assets under Reg. § 1.704-1(b)(2)(iv)(f), or

   b. The partnership does elect to revalue its assets under the regulations.

2. If W had purchased X's interest in the partnership instead of acquiring an interest through a contribution to the partnership, would the partnership be permitted to revalue its assets under the regulations? Why or why not?

Chapter Five
Substantial Economic Effect

Assignment:

Logic: Chapter Five

Code: §§ 704(b), 761(c)

Regulations: §§ 1.704-1(b)(1), (2) [omit (iv)(e), (j)-(q)], (3), (4)(i), Prop. Regs. § 1.704-1(b)(1)

Recommended Reading: *Orrisch v. Commissioner*, 55 T.C. 395 (1970).

Introductory Note.

The general idea behind § 704(a) is simple to state: partners are free to define their business relationship as they see fit. In principle, how they assign the risks and rewards of the partnership business among themselves is none of the government's business. Their assignment of the risks and rewards is legally fixed in the contract that controls their relationship: the partnership agreement. The tax law will respect their economic arrangement embodied in the partnership agreement.

The general idea behind § 704(b) also is simple to state: allocations of the partnership's tax items – income, gain, deduction, and loss – must conform to the partners' economic arrangement. To the extent that the allocations do not, the tax items will be reallocated so as to conform to the economic arrangement. This idea is succinctly expressed in Reg. § 1.704-1(b)(2)(i)(a):

> *Fundamental principles.* In order for an allocation to have economic effect, it must be consistent with the underlying economic arrangement of the partners. This means that in the event there is an economic benefit or economic burden that corresponds to an allocation, the partner to whom the allocation is made must receive such economic benefit or economic burden.

Some people think that the § 704(b) regulations could have ended right there (although a few words would have been needed on the substantiality point), without sacrificing any effectiveness whatever. That did not happen. These regulations are long, detailed, and the most complex of the regulations interpreting subchapter K. Before examining these regulations more closely consider the following Preliminary Question:

Building sold at the beg. of year 3.

Preliminary Question:

A and B, calendar year individuals, are partners in the AB general partnership to which they each contributed $100 cash. Their interests under the partnership agreement are as follows:

	A's percentages	B's percentages
Capital	50	50
Profits	60	40
Losses	30	70

Capital accounts (including deficit restoration obligations) will be followed in making all distributions, both current and liquidating.

During the first year of operations, AB loses $100. In the second year of operations, AB loses $100. In the third year of operations, AB has $200 of net income. Please prepare a balance sheet that reflects the situation at the end of each of the three years of operation.

(a) How would AB allocate profits and losses for the first three years of operations?

(b) If AB were to liquidate at the end, alternatively, of each of the first three years of operations, who would receive what?

(c) What if, in June of Year 3, when it looks as though AB will earn about $200, A and B amend the partnership agreement to adjust their profit shares for Year 3 only: A goes from 60% to 30%; B goes from 40% to 70%. What effect might that have on your conclusions about the allocation of tax losses in years 1 and 2 and the allocation of bottom line income in Year 3?

Problems:

1.   G and L organize the GL partnership. Each contributes $50 for his partnership interest. The partnership purchases an apartment building for $1,000, making a $100 down payment and paying the remainder of the price with a mortgage loan. The principal of the mortgage loan is payable in a single payment after 12 years. The gross income and deductions of the partnership for each of the first few years are expected to be as follows:

Rent		$240
Cash operating expenses	$150	
Interest expense	90	
Depreciation expense	50	
		($290)
Loss		($ 50)

The partnership agreement allocates all depreciation deductions to L. All other gross income and deductions are allocated to the partners equally.

The partnership agreement provides that all income, gains, losses and deductions will be reflected in the partners' capital accounts (which will be maintained in accordance with Reg. § 1.704-1(b)(2)(iv)); and each partner will be entitled on liquidation (of either the partnership or the partner's interest) to distribution of an amount equal to his positive capital account balance.

Assume that the partnership operates for two years, and then sells the building at the end of year 2 for, alternatively, $1,100 or $800. How will the partnership's income, gain, loss and deduction (including depreciation deductions) be allocated between G and L, and will the allocations be respected for federal income tax purposes, in the following alternative variations?

(a)   The partnership is a general partnership, the mortgage lender has full recourse against the partnership and the partners, and any partner having a deficit in his capital account when either the partnership or his interest is liquidated must then make an additional capital contribution equal to that deficit.

b)   The partnership is a limited partnership with G as the general partner and L as the limited partner; the mortgage loan is recourse; and the partnership agreement says nothing about capital account deficit restoration on liquidation of a partner's interest.

(c)   Same as (b), except L is obligated to restore any deficit in his capital account to the extent that it does not exceed $50, and there is a "QIO" provision [within the meaning of Reg. § 1.704-1(b)(2)(ii)(d)] in the partnership agreement.

> (i) Would the year 2 allocations have economic effect or alternate economic effect if: (1) as of the end of year 2 of operations, the partnership plans in year 3 to borrow $60 on a recourse basis and distribute the cash proceeds of the loan equally to G and L, and (2) the partnership reasonably expects to earn $60 net income in year 3?
>
> (ii) What if, in year 3, the partnership borrows $60 and distributes $30 to each of G and L as planned, but unexpectedly earns only $40 (net income)?

(d)   **Note: Do after Question #3.** Same as (a) except the partnership agreement has a "gain charge-back provision", i.e., a provision that allocates to L all gain on a sale of the apartment building up to the aggregate amount of the depreciation taken on the property.

2. The AB partnership agreement satisfies the three basic requirements of the economic effect test of Reg. § 1.704-1(b)(2)(ii)(b). The AB partnership owns a portfolio of municipal bonds and a AAA Corporate bond with a variable rate of interest. At the beginning of last year, each investment had a value of $1,000 and each was expected to yield approximate income of $60. The partnership had net operating income from its business of $300 for the year. How will the tax exempt and taxable interest be allocated to the partners if the partnership agreement provides:

(a) A and B share equally in aggregate partnership income but A's share is deemed to consist first of interest on the municipal bonds? Assume that the bonds generate the expected amount of income of $60 each.

(b) A and B share equally in operating income but the interest on the municipal bonds is allocated solely to A and the taxable interest are allocated solely to B? Assume alternatively:

(i) The agreement on the allocation of interest is made before the beginning of last year and the municipal bonds and corporate bond in fact earn $60 each of interest, as expected. At the time the agreement is made, A and B are both in the 40% marginal bracket, but B has substantial investment interest carryovers under § 163(d).

(ii) The same as (i), except B had no investment interest carryover. However, during the year B incurred substantial investment interest expense.

(iii) Same as (i) but as it turns out the municipal bonds earn $60 interest and the corporate bond earns $80 in interest.

3. X and Y form a partnership solely to purchase equipment for leasing. The cost of the equipment is $1,000. X and Y each contribute $50 to the partnership and the partnership obtains a $900 recourse loan to purchase the equipment. The partnership enters into an 8-year net lease with a financially sound lessee. Because the equipment is 5-year property for purposes of § 168, the partnership expects to have tax losses for the first 3 years of its operations of $100, $100, and $50 respectively. For the remaining five years of the initial lease, it expects to generate taxable profits of $75, $75, $100, $100 and $100.

The XY partnership agreement satisfies the three basic requirements of the economic effect test of Reg. § 1.704-1(b)(2)(ii)(b). The partnership allocates 90% of all partnership income and losses to X and 10% to Y until such time as the amount of taxable income that has been allocated to the partners equals the amount of previously allocated tax losses. Thereafter, all partnership allocations will be allocated 50-50.

On the assumptions that Y is at all relevant times in the 35% tax bracket and that X has an NOL that will expire in three years, will these allocations be respected?

13

Chapter Six
Allocation of Nonrecourse Deductions

Assignment:

Logic: Chapter Six

Regulations: §§ 1.704-2(b)-(j), (m) Ex. (1) [omit part (v)]; skim § 1.752-3(a).

Recommended Reading: *Commissioner v. Tufts*, 461 U.S. 300 (1983).

Optional Reading: Laura E. Cunningham and Noël B. Cunningham, *The Story of Tufts: The 'Logic' of Taxing Nonrecourse Transactions in* BUSINESS TAX STORIES (Foundation Press 2005)

Problem

On January 1, 2004, G and L form a limited partnership to acquire and operate a rental apartment building. L, the limited partner, contributes $90 and G, the general partner, $10. The partnership obtains a nonrecourse loan from an unrelated financial institution for $900 and purchases a building (on leased land) for $1,000. The loan is secured by the building. The loan requires interest to be paid currently, but does not call for any principal payment for 5 years. The building is depreciable over 10 years at the rate of $100 per year.

The partnership agreement contains the following provisions:

1. The agreement satisfies the alternate test for economic effect under § 1.704-1(b)(2)(ii)(d), i.e., it contains the requisite provisions for capital account maintenance and distribution of liquidation proceeds. Although G has a deficit makeup obligation L does not, but the agreement includes a "QIO" provision.
2. The agreement includes a "minimum gain chargeback" provision that complies with § 1.704-2(f).
3. All income and loss, <u>other than nonrecourse deductions</u>, are allocated 90% to L and 10% to G until the first time that the partnership recognizes income and gain that exceed losses sustained in prior years. Thereafter, all income, gain and loss are allocated 50% to G and 50% to L.
4. Nonrecourse deductions are allocated 80% to L and 20% to G.
5. Non-liquidating cash distributions are divided 10% to G and 90% to L until they have each recovered their initial capital contributions (i.e., $10 to G and $90 to L). Thereafter, all non-liquidating cash distributions are to be shared 50%-50%.

For the taxable years 2004-06, the partnership has rental income of $70, operating expenses of $10, interest expense of $60, and a cost recovery deduction of $100, for a net loss of $100.

Questions:

(a) Is the 80/20 split of nonrecourse deductions permissible? How much flexibility do G and L have to allocate partnership nonrecourse deductions? Specifically, which of the following would be permissible?

	G	L
(i)	50%	50%
(ii)	10%	90%
(iii)	1%	99%

(b) Assume that on January 1, 2007 the partnership defaults on the mortgage and transfers the building (then worth $600) to the lender by deed in lieu of foreclosure, and liquidates. What are the appropriate tax allocations and cash distributions to G and L for 2004, 2005, 2006 and 2007?

(c) What if, instead, on January 1 2007 the partnership sells the building for $1,100 and liquidates. What are the appropriate tax allocations and distributions to G and L?

(d) What if, instead, in 2006 the partnership borrows an additional $100, using the building as security, and distributes the cash to the partners in the ratio of 10/90, in accordance with the partnership agreement. What is the aggregate partnership minimum gain at the end of the year, and what is each partner's share of PMG? If the partnership then sells the building on January 1, 2007 what are the appropriate allocations and distributions?

doesn't include dep'r.

(e) What if in part (c) instead of selling the building in 2007, the partnership continues to operate throughout 2007, during which it earns net income of $600. It then sells the building on January 1, 2008 and liquidates. What are the appropriate allocations and distributions? *just enough to cover losses then 50/50*

(f) Suppose that in part (c) on January 1, 2006 G and L contribute cash to the partnership in the amounts of $40 and $160, respectively, and the partnership uses these contributions to reduce the balance of the mortgage from $900 to $700. What tax consequences occur in 2006 as a result of these transactions?

(g) What difference would it make in part (a) if G had guaranteed the original $900 loan to the lender?

Chapter Seven
Contributions of Property

Assignment:

Logic: Chapter Seven

Code: § 704(c)(1)(A), (C).

Regulations: § 1.704-3(a)(1)-(7), (b), (c), (d).

Problems:

Unless otherwise indicated, in each of the following problems you should assume that the relevant partnership agreement complies with the basic test for economic effect under Reg. § 1.704-1(b)(2)(ii).

A. Contributions of Non-Depreciable Property

On January 1 of the current year A and B form a partnership to invest in property. A contributes investment land that she acquired two years ago, and that has a fair market value of $100. B contributes $100 in cash. Each partner receives a 50% interest in the partnership's capital, profits and losses.

1. Pre-Contribution Gain. For purposes of Problem 1, assume that A's basis in the land at the time she contributed it to the partnership is $50

(a)   Under the "traditional method" of accounting for § 704(c) gain, how will the partnership allocate its gain or loss for *book and tax* purposes if the partnership sells the land for:

      i. $100
      ii. $150
      iii. $ 70
      iv. $ 30

(b)   Assume the partnership invests B's cash in stock that appreciates and the partnership sells the stock in the same taxable year in which it sells the land: would your answer to (a)(iii) above differ if the partnership used the "traditional method with curative allocations?"

(c)   What if, in (b), the partnership does not sell the stock and, in fact, has no items of income, gain, loss or deduction in the year that the land is sold other than from the sale of the land: would your answer to (a)(iii) above differ if the partnership used the "traditional method with curative allocations?"

(d)   How would your answer to (a)(iii) differ if the partnership used the "remedial allocation method"?

2. Pre-Contribution Loss. For purposes of Problem 2, assume that A's basis in the land at the time of contribution is $140. Under the "traditional method", how will the partnership allocate its gain or loss for book and tax purposes if the partnership sells the land for:

(a) $70
(b) $120
(c) $160

B. Contributions of Depreciable Property

Five years ago, A acquired equipment to use in her leasing business. The equipment had a recovery period of 10 years and A elected to use straight line depreciation. On January 1 of this year, A formed an equipment leasing partnership with B. A contributed the equipment with a fair market value of $100 and B contributed $100 in cash. A and B agreed to share all profits and losses equally. The partnership will maintain the partners' capital accounts according to Reg. § 1.704-1(b)(2)(iv). The equipment would have had a 10 year recovery period if the partnership had purchased the equipment this year. Each year the partnership will have gross rental income of $20 before taking into account depreciation. The partnership will have no other income and no expenses other than depreciation.

1. Traditional Method. Under the "traditional method", how will the partnership allocate each year's depreciation on the equipment for *book and tax* purposes if A's basis in the equipment (at the time of contribution) was, alternatively:

(a) $80
(b) $120
(c) $50
(d) $20

2. Curative Allocations. Assume in problem 1(d) above that B insisted that the partnership use the "traditional method with curative allocations".

(a) Would curative allocations affect the partners' 50-50 allocations of "book" items for purposes of Reg. § 1.704-1(b)(2)(iv)?

(b) How would the partnership allocate its $20 per year of gross rental income and its tax depreciation?

3. Remedial Allocations. What result in 1(d) above if B insisted that the partnership use the "remedial allocation method?"

C. Reverse § 704(c) Transactions

Several years ago A and B formed a partnership that acquired an apartment building to rent. A and B are equal partners. On the first day of the current year, when the building has a value of $120 and the partnership's adjusted tax basis in the building is $40, A and B admit C as a one-third partner in exchange for a $60 cash contribution.

1. No Revaluation. Assume that the partnership did not choose to revalue, or "book up" its capital accounts to fair market value upon admission of C. Determine how the partnership should allocate its $80 of tax and book gain if the property were sold for $120. If your answer is an equal one third division of the gain, might any of the partners object to that result? Why? What other alternative does the partnership have? See § 704(c), the last sentence of § 1.704-1(b)(2)(iv)(f) and § 1.704-1(b)(1)(iii) and (iv).

2. Revaluation. Assume that the partnership revalues its capital accounts as permitted by Reg. § 1.704-1(b)(2)(iv)(f) to reflect fair market value of the building as of C's admission, and elects to use the traditional method for allocations with respect to the revalued property. Reconstruct the partnership's balance sheet.

(a) **Gain allocation.** If the building is subsequently sold at a time that its basis is still $40, how would the partnership allocate the resulting book and tax gain or loss if the building is sold, in the alternative, for:

(i) $120
(ii) $90
(iii) $15

(b) **Depreciation allocation.** Assume the partnership will recover the remaining $40 tax basis in the building at the rate of $10 per year over the building's remaining 4 year life under ACRS. How will the partnership allocate those deductions if it uses the traditional method for making § 704(c) allocations?

Chapter Eight
Partnership Liabilities

Assignment:

Logic: Chapter Eight

Code: §§ 704(d), § 705(a), 722, 731(a)(1), 733, 752

Regulations: §§ 1.704-1(d), 1.704-1(b)(2)(iv)(c), 1.731-1(a)(1), 1.752-0 thru -4.

Recommended Reading: *Raphan v. United States,* 3 Cl.Ct. 457 (1983), *aff'd in part, rev'd in part,* 759 F.2d 879 Fed Cir. 1985)

Problems:

1. Limitations on Losses under § 704(d).

A and B, calendar year individuals, are equal partners in a real estate partnership. In the current year, the partnership had gross rental income of $250 and deductions, including depreciation, of $300. To what extent is the resulting loss of $50 deductible by the partners limited under § 704(d), if:

(a)   The adjusted bases of A and B for their interests in the partnership as of the last day of the current year (after adjustment for all events during the year other than the loss) are $10 and $30, respectively.

(b)   Same as (a) except the partnership has taxable income of $30 for the following year.

(c)   Same as (a) except the current year's loss is comprised of an operating loss of $30 and a long-term capital loss of $20?

(d)   Same as (a) except that A's basis at the beginning of the year was $10, A contributed an additional $10 to partnership capital at the middle of the year, and the partnership distributed $20 to him on the last day of the year.

2. Economic Risk of Loss: Allocating Recourse Liabilities of a General Partnership

A and B organized a general partnership in the current year to acquire and develop a tract of land. Each contributed $20 to the partnership for a 50 percent interest in capital, profits and losses. The partnership purchased the land from a third party for $200. It paid the price with the funds contributed by the partners and a mortgage loan of $160. Assume under local law that A and B are each jointly and severally liable to repay the mortgage, including interest, if the partnership cannot pay it. The partnership agreement contains the appropriate capital account deficit restoration provisions.

(a)　　The partnership engaged in no transactions during the year other than the purchase of the land. What is the basis of each partner's interest at the end of current year?

(b)　　Would it make any difference in (a) if the partnership had borrowed the $160 from A or had purchased the property from A on a deferred payment basis, in each case giving A its $160 recourse obligation?

(c)　　Same as (a), except that A contributed $40 and B contributed no initial capital, but they still agree to share profits and losses equally.

3. Defining and Sharing Recourse Liabilities of a Limited Partnership

The GL limited partnership was organized at the beginning of the current year. G, the general partner, contributed $10 for a 10 percent interest in profits, losses and capital, and L, as limited partner, received a 90 percent interest in profits, losses and capital in exchange for a capital contribution of $90. The partnership immediately purchased a rental apartment building for $1,000, paying $100 in cash and issuing a $900 purchase money note, with interest payable currently and a lump-sum principal payment due in 20 years. Determine each partner's initial outside basis under each of the following alternatives:

(a)　　The note is recourse, and hence the partnership (and G as its general partner) is personally liable on the note. As a limited partner, L is required to make no additional capital contributions beyond the $90 he contributed upon formation. L has no personal liability with respect to the note.

(b)　　Same as (a), except that under the partnership agreement L, as the limited partner, is obligated to contribute additional capital of $900 to the partnership in the future (making the total required capital from L $990).

(c)　　Same as (a), except that L has assumed and promised to pay the entire note as it becomes due. Assume that the holder of the mortgage could proceed directly against L as well as G and the partnership if the note is not paid. Also assume that if the holder of the mortgage sued G or the partnership for payment, G and the partnership would sue L for the same amount since L's assumption made him ultimately liable on the debt.

(d)　　Same as (a), except that L has guaranteed the note in a side agreement directly with the holder of the mortgage?

4. Defining and Sharing Nonrecourse liabilities.

Assume that the $900 note in problem 3 is nonrecourse (i.e., it is secured by the apartment building but neither the partnership nor either of its partners has any personal liability on the note).

(a) Determine each partner's initial outside basis in the partnership.

(b) Same as (a), except that L pledged IBM stock (basis $100, value $200) to secure the loan?

(c) Same as (a), except that L guaranteed the note in a side agreement with the holder?

(d) **(Not to be covered in class unless specifically assigned):** Same as (a), except that the partnership's note is guaranteed, alternatively, by:

      i.   G's wholly owned corporation?
      ii.   L's father?
      iii.   G's sister?
      iv.   Another partnership in which L is an 80% partner? or
      v.   A partner of L in another partnership?

(e) Same as (a), except that the apartment building was previously owned by G and was contributed by him to the partnership at a time when its value was $910, its tax basis was $110, and it was subject to a $900 nonrecourse note? Assume that L's contribution is used to pay operating expenses. The partnership books up the apartment building to its $910 value upon contribution by G, and the capital accounts of G and L are credited at $10 and $90, respectively. Is there more than one possible correct answer?

Chapter Nine
Partner/Partnership Transactions

Part A. Payments to a Partner under §§ 707(a) and 707(c)

Assignment:

Logic: Chapter Nine, pp. 125-133

Code: §§ 707(a)(1), (a)(2)(A), (c), 267(a)(2), (e)(1)-(4).

Regulations: §§ 1.707-1(a), (c); 1.704-1(b)(1)(v), (2)(iv)(o).

Problems:

1. A is a partner in the ABC partnership. Under the partnership agreement A is entitled to $10,000 each year for his services, which are ordinary in nature and performed in his capacity as a partner. A's share of the partnership's profits and losses, after deduction of the services payment, is one third. For 2007 the partnership's income, before deduction of the $10,000 payment to A, consisted of $4,000 of ordinary income and $15,000 of long-term capital gain. A and the partnership use the calendar year as their taxable years. A is a cash method taxpayer, and the partnership uses the accrual method.

(a) Determine partnership taxable income for 2007 and A's distributive share.

(b) When is the $10,000 included in A's gross income if it is paid to him on January 3, 2008?

(c) How does A's entitlement to the $10,000 and the payment of this sum affect the basis of his interest?

2. In the alternative, assume that A is to receive one third of partnership profits (regardless of character) but not less than $10,000 (this minimum guarantee to be financed from B's and C's accounts). Determine partnership taxable income and A's distributable share of the same if partnership income for 2007 consisted of:

(a)   Ordinary income of $15,000 and long-term capital gains of $15,000,

(b)   Ordinary income of $15,000, or

(c)   Ordinary income of $6,000.

3. X and Y plan to construct a mall. They have hired an architect (Z) to design the project, whose fee would normally be $100,000. X and Y propose that, in lieu of

paying Z her normal fee, she receive an interest in the partnership in exchange for her services. Z's interest would entitle her to 8% of the partnership's gross income for its first three years of operations, at which point her interest in the partnership would terminate. X and Y have obtained signed lease agreements for most of the project, which will generate approximately $400,000 of gross rental income per year. What might be the advantage of organizing the venture in this way? Will it work?

Part B. Partnership Interests in Exchange for Services

Assignment:

Logic: pp. 133-38

Code: Skim §§ 83(a), (b) & (h)

Regulations: Prop. Regs. §§ 1.721-1(b)(1)-(5); 1.83-3(e) & (l)

Recommended Reading: Diamond v. Commissioner, 492 F.2d 286 (7th Cir. 1974); *Rev. Proc. 2001-43*, 2001-2 C.B. 191

Optional Reading: Victor Fleischer, *Two and Twenty: Taxing Partnership Profits in Private Equity Funds*, 83 NYU L. Rev. 1. (2008).

Problems:

1. A, B and C decide to form a partnership for the purpose of developing real property. A and B are wealthy individuals, with no particular real estate experience. C is an experienced developer. The parties agree that A and B will each contribute $1,000,000 to the venture, and that C will contribute his expertise. What tax consequences will result from formation of the venture under each of the following alternatives?

   (a) In exchange for cash contributions of $1,000,000 apiece, A and B each receive a forty percent interest in the profits, losses and capital of the venture. In exchange for his future services C receives the remaining 20% interest in profits, losses and capital.

   (b) In exchange for their cash contributions A and B each receive a 50% interest in capital and losses. Profits of the venture are divided 40% to A, 40% to B, and 20% to C.

   (c) What if in (a) instead of contributing cash, A and B jointly contribute a piece of raw land that they have held for investment for several years. The property is worth $2,000,000, and it has a basis of $100,000.

   (d) Would your answer to part (c) differ if A and B form a partnership in year one, and admit C as a partner in year three?

2. Five years ago T created a partnership to operate a fund to invest in various private enterprises. He raised $95 million from limited partners and invested $5 million of his own. T is the sole general partner. The partnership agreement provides that T will receive, as compensation for his services as general partner, (i) an annual management fee equal to 2% of the initial capital of the fund, ($2,000,000 per year) and (ii) 20% of the fund's profits (defined as realized gains). Net profits, i.e., realized gains minus T's 20% share, are divided among the partners in proportion to capital contributions.

The fund has been successful and this year it sold one of the stocks in its portfolio for a long term capital gain of $50 million. As a result, T receives the following in the current year:

    (i) $2,000,000 as his annual management fee.

    (ii) $10,000,000 as his 20% profit share

    (iii) $2,000,000 as his 5% share of the net profits that he receives as a result of his 5% capital contribution.

How will T be taxed on each of these amounts?

Chapter Ten
Sales of Partnership Interests

Part A: Consequences to Sellers

Assignment:

Logic: Chapter Ten, pp. 139-146

Code: §§ 1(h)(6), 741, 751(a), (c), (d), 453(i).

Regulations: §§ 1.1(h)-1, 1.741-1; 1.751-1(a), (c), (d), (e), (g) ex.(1).

Recommended Reading: Ledoux v. Commissioner, 77 T.C. 293 (1981), *aff'd per curiam,*
695 F.2d 1320 (11th Cir. 1983)

Problems:

1. A, B and C are equal partners in the ABC partnership. On January 1, 2000,
A's outside basis is $250 and ABC's balance sheet (including FMV's) is as follows:

Assets			Liabilities & Capital	
	AB/Book	**FMV**	**Liabilities**	
Cash	$240	$240	$150	
Accts Rec.	75	60		
Inventory	90	150		
Machinery	55	100		
Building	200	500		
Stock	90	300		
Goodwill	0	300		
Total	$750	$1650		

		Capital Accounts	
		Tax/Book	*FMV*
	A	$200	$500
	B	200	500
	C	200	500
	Total	$600	$1500

a. What are the tax consequences to A if A were to sell her interest to P for $500
cash? Assume that ABC purchased the machine three years ago for $120, and
that $120 in depreciation has been taken on the building since its acquisition
five years ago.

b. What difference would it make, if any, if P paid A $200 in cash at closing and gave A her note for the balance of $300 (bearing adequate stated interest)? **Do not do the calculations.**

Part B: Consequences to Buyers

Assignment:

Logic: Chapter Ten, pp. 147-157

Code: §§ 732(a) & (d), 742, 743(a-(d), 754, 755(a) & (b).

Regulations: §§ 1.704-1(b)(2)(iv)(l), (m)(1), (2) & (5); 1.704-1(b)(5) Ex. (13)(iii) & (iv), 1.742-1, 1.743-1(a)-(e) & (j), 1.754-1, 1.755-1(a)(1) & (b)(1)-(3).

Problems:

1. P purchased the 1/3 interest from A **Problem 1** in **Part A** above for $500 cash. What is P's initial outside basis and the balance in her capital account at the time of purchase?

2. In the absence of a § 754 election, what would be the tax consequences to P if she P held the interest for three years and then sold it for $500. Assume that during this period of time the partnership engaged in no transactions and there was no change in the value of its assets (ignore cost recovery allowances).

3. If an election under § 754 is made,

    (i)   What is the amount of the § 743(b) adjustment and how should it be allocated among the partnership's assets?

    (ii)   Is this adjustment reflected in P's "book" capital account under Reg. § 1.704-1(b)(2)(iv)(m)(2)?

    (iii)   How should the partnership compute its cost recovery allowance on the building and the machinery for the year of P's purchase and thereafter?

4. What difference would it make to your answer to 3(i) if A had contributed the stock to the partnership when its value was $180? [Assume also for this purpose that the partnership's basis in the building was $110, this adjustment to the facts is arbitrary and is done simply to maintain equality

between inside and outside basis] If this were the case then at the time of the sale, A's outside basis would be $160 and the partnership's capital accounts would be as follows:

	Tax	Book	FMV
A	$110	$200	$500
B	$200	$200	$500
C	$200	$200	$500
	$510	$600	$1500

Part C: Shifting Partnership Interests

Assignment:

Logic: Chapter Ten, pp.157-159

Code: §§ 706(c) & (d).

Regulations: §§ 1.706-1(c)(1), (2) & (4).

Problem:

A, an individual whose taxable year is the calendar year, is a one-third partner in the ABC partnership, which uses the accrual method of accounting and reports on a fiscal year ending June 30. The partnership's taxable income for the year ending June 30, 2007 is $36,000. How will the taxable income allocable to A's interest ($12,000) be reported if:

(a) A sells her entire interest to P on December 31, 2006? Would it make a difference whether the partnership (i) earned its income ratably over the year or (ii) earned all of the income in the first six months of the year (July 1 through December 31) and broke even during the last six months?

(b) A sells one-half of his interest to P on December 31, 2006?

Chapter Eleven
Distributions: The Basics

Part A: Prorata Current Distributions

Assignment:

Logic: Chapter Eleven

Code: §§ 731(a) & (b), 732(a) & (c); 733; 734(a), 735.

Regulations: §§ 1.704-1(b)(2)(iv)(e), -1(b)(5) Ex.(14)(v); 1.731-1(a)(1), (3), -1(c);
               1.732-1(a), (c); 1.752-1(e), (f).

Problem:

ABC is a cash-method partnership with three equal partners, A, B and C. It has no liabilities. Its assets are:

	Basis	**FMV**
Cash	$ 60	$ 60
Inventory	60	90
Acc'ts Receivable[1]	0	30
Land held for investment	30	90
Total	$150	$270

Assume the bases of A, B and C for their partnership interests are $40, $30 and $20, respectively. The partnership's total inside basis exceeds the partners' total outside bases, even though the partnership assets reflect unrealized appreciation. (Can you figure out how this might happen? See footnote[2] for one possibility).

What are the tax consequences to the partnership and the partners if the partnership:

(a)   Makes a cash distribution of $20 to each partner and also distributes an undivided one-third interest in the land to each partner,

(b)   Makes a distribution to each partner consisting of $10 in cash, one-third of the inventory and an undivided one-third interest in the land,

---

[1] Reg. § 1.446-1(c)(2)(i) requires use of the accrual method for purchases and sales if the taxpayer must maintain inventories. Assume the receivables in the problem arose from a separate business carried on by the partnership, unrelated to its inventory sales, for which the cash method is used. See Reg § 1.446-1(d).

[2] One possibility is that one or more of the partners bought her or their interest(s) when the partnership assets had declined in value to less than the partnership's basis (i.e., when the partnership had unrealized losses); no § 754 election was in effect; and the asset values subsequently rebounded.

(c)   Makes a distribution to each partner consisting of $10 in cash, one-third of the accounts receivable, and one-third of the inventory, or

(d)   Distributes $45 cash to A and distributes one-half undivided interests in the land to B and C.

(e)   *Do only if specifically assigned:* Borrows $75, giving a mortgage on the land as security, distributes the land (subject to the mortgage) to A, and distributes $15 in cash to each of B and C.

Part B: Prorata Liquidating Distributions

Assignment:

Code: §§ 731(a), (b) & (d); 732(b) & (c); 735; 761(d).

Regulations::   §§ 1.706-1(c)(2); 1.731-1(a); 1.732-1(a)-(c); 1.761-1(d).

Problem:

ABC is an equal partnership. On January 1, 2005, A's outside basis is $170 and the partnership's balance sheet is as follows (expanded to include fair market values):

	AB/Book	FMV	Liabilities
Cash	$120	$120	$150
Accts Rec.	0	30	
Inventory	30	60	
Land #1	180	120	
Land #2	90	120	
Stock (non-marketable	90	150	
Total	$510	$600	

		Capital Accounts	
		Tax/Book	FMV
	A	$120	$150
	B	120	150
	C	120	150
	Total	$360	$450

On this date, A receives the following *alternative* distributions in complete liquidation of her interest in the partnership. What are the tax consequences to A as a result of each of these distributions?

1. The accounts receivable and Land #1.

2. The accounts receivable and Land #2.

3. One-half the inventory and Land #1.

4. One-third of both the inventory and the accounts receivables and Land #2.

5. The accounts receivable and a one-half interest in both Land #1 and Land #2.

6. One-third of both the inventory and the accounts receivables and $120 cash.

    i.   What difference would it make if A's outside basis were only $100?

    ii. What difference would it make if A's outside basis were $200?

Chapter Twelve
Optional Basis Adjustment

Part A: **Effects of Distributions on Adjusted Bases of Undistributed Assets**

Assignment:

Logic: Chapter Twelve

Code: §§ 734; 754; 755.

Regulations: §§ 1.704-1(b)(2)(iv)(m)(1), (4) & (5); 1.734-1, -2; 1.754-1; 1.755-1(a) & (c).

Problems:

1. ABC is an equal partnership that has made a § 754 election. On January 1, 2007, A's outside basis is $2100 and the partnership's balance sheet is as follows (expanded to include fair market values (000's omitted)):

Assets			Liabilities & Capital	
	AB/Book	*FMV*	*Liabilities*	
Cash	$3000	$3000	$1500	
Accts Rec.	0	300		
Inventory	300	600		
Blackacre	1500	1200		
Whiteacre	600	1200		
Greenacre	900	1500		
Total	$6300	$7800		

			Capital Accounts	
			Tax/Book	*FMV*
		A	$1600	$2100
		B	1600	2100
		C	1600	2100
		Total	$4800	$6300

On this date, the partnership makes the following alternative distributions in liquidation of A's interest in the partnership. Please determine the basis that A takes in each of the assets she receives, and the adjustments (if any) that the partnership must make to the each of its retained assets.

a. A receives $600 cash, the accounts receivable and Blackacre.

b. A receives $600 cash, ½ the inventory, and Whiteacre.

c. A receives $300 cash, the accounts receivables, and Greenacre.

d. A receives $1800 in cash and the receivables.

2. What difference would it make in Question #1(c), if there were no § 754 election in place at the time of the distribution?

3. Assume in the alternative that ABC had not fared so well and that on January 1, 2007 A's outside basis was $3200 and the partnership's balance sheet were as follows (expanded to include fair market values (000's omitted)):

<table>
<tr><td colspan="3">Assets</td><td colspan="3">Liabilities & Capital</td></tr>
<tr><td></td><td>AB/Book</td><td>FMV</td><td colspan="3">Liabilities</td></tr>
<tr><td>Cash</td><td>$2900</td><td>$2900</td><td>$1500</td><td></td><td></td></tr>
<tr><td>Accts Rec.</td><td>0</td><td>300</td><td></td><td></td><td></td></tr>
<tr><td>Inventory</td><td>400</td><td>600</td><td></td><td></td><td></td></tr>
<tr><td>Blackacre</td><td>2900</td><td>1400</td><td></td><td></td><td></td></tr>
<tr><td>Whiteacre</td><td>900</td><td>1100</td><td></td><td></td><td></td></tr>
<tr><td>Greenacre</td><td>2500</td><td>1500</td><td></td><td></td><td></td></tr>
<tr><td>Total</td><td>$9600</td><td>$7800</td><td></td><td></td><td></td></tr>
<tr><td></td><td></td><td></td><td></td><td colspan="2">Capital Accounts</td></tr>
<tr><td></td><td></td><td></td><td></td><td>Tax/Book</td><td>FMV</td></tr>
<tr><td></td><td></td><td></td><td>A</td><td>$2700</td><td>$2100</td></tr>
<tr><td></td><td></td><td></td><td>B</td><td>2700</td><td>2100</td></tr>
<tr><td></td><td></td><td></td><td>C</td><td>2700</td><td>2100</td></tr>
<tr><td></td><td></td><td></td><td>Total</td><td>$8100</td><td>$6300</td></tr>
</table>

On this date, A receives the following alternative liquidating distributions in complete liquidation of A's interest in the partnership. Please determine the basis that A takes in each of the assets she receives, and the adjustments (if any) that the partnership must make to the each of its retained assets.

a. A receives $1800 in cash and the accounts receivable.

b. A receives $400 in cash, the accounts receivable and Blackacre.

Part B: Sales of Distributed Property

Assignment:

Code: §§ 732(d); 735; 7701(a)(42) - (45).

Regulations: §§ 1.704-1(b)(2)(iv)(m)(1) & (3); 1.732-1(d); -2; 1.735-1.

Problems:

     1.   A and B, neither of whom are in the real estate business in their individual capacities, are equal partners in a partnership which regularly develops and sells lots for home building. The partnership distributes to A a lot with a basis in excess of its value, and to B a lot with a value in excess of its basis. A plans to sell his lot and recognize an ordinary loss, whereas B plans to give his lot to his son who will sell it and recognize a long-term capital gain. Will the plan work?

     2.   D purchased from A a one-third interest in the profits and capital of the ABC partnership for $60. The assets of the partnership then consisted of subdivision lots held for sale to customers in the ordinary course of the partnership business (value, $90, adjusted basis, $60) and a tract of land held for investment (value $90, basis $30). The partnership had no liabilities. What are the tax consequences to D if, alternatively:

    (a) The partnership makes a § 754 election for the year in which D bought his interest; within two years after D's purchase, the partnership distributes an undivided one third interest in the lots to each of the partners; and D sells the interest he receives for $30.

    (b) What if, in (a), the partnership makes no § 754 election?

    (c) What if, in (b), the distribution were made more than two years after D's purchase?

(d) What if the partnership makes no § 754 election and, within two years after D's purchase, D sells his partnership interest for $60 before the partnership engages in any transactions or the values of its assets change? See § 751(a).

Chapter Thirteen
Disproportionate Distributions

Assignment:

Logic: Chapter Thirteen

Code: §§ 732(e); 751(b).

Regulations: §§ 1.731-1(b); 1.732-1(e); 1.751-1(b), -1(g) exs. (2) thru (4)

Recommended Reading: Rev. Rul. 84-102, 1984-2 C.B. 119

Problems:

1. ABC is an equal partnership in which each partner has an outside basis and capital account balance of $1000. On January 1 of this year, the partnership's balance sheet is as follows:

	Book	*FMV*
Inventory	$1800	$6000
Capital Asset	1200	3000
	$3000	$9000

	Capital	*Accounts*
	Book	*FMV*
A	$1000	$3000
B	1000	3000
C	1000	3000
	$3000	$9000

On this date, ABC distributes the Capital Asset to A in complete liquidation of her interest in the partnership.

a. In the absence of § 751(b), what would be the tax consequences of this distribution to the various parties? What might Congress find these results objectionable?

b. Taking into account § 751(b), what are the tax consequences to the partnership and each of the partners?

2. A owns 50% of the ABC general partnership. The remaining 50% is owned equally by B and C. The partnership made a § 754 election. Prior to any distributions, A's outside basis is $550. On January 1, 2004, ABC distributes Land with a value of $400 in complete liquidation of her interest in the partnership. At the time of the liquidating distribution the partnership's balance sheet (after booking up) is as follows:

	Assets			*Liabilities & Capital*	
	Basis	*Book*	*Liabilities*		
Inventory	$100	$240	Mortgage		$900
Land	250	400			
Building	750	1060			
Total	$1100	$1700			

	Capital Accounts	
	Tax	*Book*
A	$100	$400
B	50	200
C	50	200
Total	$200	$800

Questions:

a. What is the amount and character of any gain or loss recognized by each of the parties as a result of this transaction?

b. What is A's basis in the land received in the transaction?

c. What is the partnership's basis in the inventory and the building after the transaction?

3. A, B and C comprise a partnership organized several years ago to invest in and develop land. Each partner contributed $100 to the partnership at its inception. The partnership used this money to purchase a tract of land as an investment and to purchase a second tract and develop this second tract as a residential subdivision. The partnership has realized no income yet but plans to sell the subdivision lots later this year and to sell the land held for investment next year. Its balance sheet is as follows:

Assets			Liabilities & Capital
	Basis	*Book*	*Liabilities*
Lots	$30	$150	None
Land	270	450	
Total	$300	$600	

		Capital Accounts	
		Tax	*Book*
	A	$100	$200
	B	100	200
	C	100	200
	Total	$300	$600

A has substantial net operating loss deductions from other investments and little income to offset them. The partnership's accountant has suggested that this situation might be exploited by distributing the lots to A before they are sold. The partnership would "book-up" the capital accounts of the partners and the assets of the partnership to fair market value as permitted under Reg. § 1.704-1(b)(2)(iv)(f). A's interest in capital and future book profits would be decreased from one-third to one-ninth to reflect this disproportionate distribution. The interests of B and C in book capital and future book profits and losses would increase to four-ninths each.

a. What are the tax consequences of the distribution to the partnership, A, B and C?

b. How might the ABC partnership structure a distribution of the lots held for resale in a manner that both avoids § 751(b) and to some extent achieves the result which § 751(b) was intended to prohibit? Assume the partnership's holding of lots (total f/m/v $150; basis $30) consists of three lots, each worth $50 with bases of $15, $15, and $0 respectively.

Chapter Fourteen
Retirement and Death of Partners

Part A: Retirements

Assignment:

Logic: Chapter Fourteen, pp 206-213

Code: §§ 706(c); 707(c); 736; 761(d).

Regulations: §§ 1.706-1(c)(2); 1.707-1(c); 1.736-1.

Problem:

ABC is an equal general partnership in which capital is not a material producing factor (i.e., a service partnership). A is planning to retire. On January 1, 2008, A's outside basis is $100. The partnership has made a § 754 election. On this date, ABC's balance sheet is as follows (expanded to include goodwill and fair market values):

Assets				*Liabilities & Capital*	
	AB/Book	*FMV*		Mortgage	$150
Cash	$120	$120			
Acc'ts Rec.	0	75			
Building	90	255			
Land	90	300			
Goodwill	0	150			
	$300	$900			

		Capital Accounts	
		Tax/Bk	*FMV*
	A	$50	$250
	B	50	250
	C	50	250
		$150	$750

Assume that no principal payments are due on the mortgage until 2010. What are the tax consequences to A if, in the alternative:

1. B and C purchase A's partnership interest, each paying $125 cash.

2. The partnership makes a lump sum payment to A in the amount of $250 in complete liquidation of A's interest in the partnership, and the agreement makes no reference to partnership goodwill?

3. The partnership makes a lump sum payment to A in the amount of $250 in complete liquidation of A's interest in the partnership. Under the partnership agreement, $50 of the payment is specifically allocated to A's share of the partnership's goodwill.

4. How would your analysis in (2) change if the partnership had equipment that had inherent recapture? *Note: No calculations are necessary.*

5. How would you answer to part (2) change if the partnership agrees to pay A the $250 over time: $50 in 2008, $100 in 2009 and a final $100 in 2010? A agrees to remain personally liable on mortgage until she receives her last payment.

Part B: Death of a Partner

Assignment:

Logic: Chapter Fourteen, pp. 213-217

Code: §§ 706(c); 736; 743(b); 753; 691(a)(1), (b), (c)(1).

Regulations: §§ 1.706-1(c)(3); 1.732-1(d)(1)(i); 1.736-1(a)(6); 1.742-1; 1.753-1(a), (b).

BASIC FACTS: DEF is an equal general partnership engaged in medical practice. On January 1, 2007, D died, triggering the partnership's buy/sell agreement. Just prior to his death, D's outside basis was $130. According to the agreement, the partnership must pay D's sole beneficiary, B, $500 in liquidation of her interest in the partnership. Neither the partnership agreement nor the buy/sell agreement mentions goodwill. There is no § 754 election in place. On the date of death, DEF's balance sheet (with FMVs) was as follows:

Assets			*Liabilities & Capital*		
	AB/Book	*FMV*	*Liabilities*		$150
Cash	$120	$120			
Acc'ts Rec.	0	150			
Installment Oblig.	150	270			
Equipment	90	300			
Land	30	510			
Goodwill	0	300			
	$390	$1650			
			Capital Accounts		
				Tax/Bk	*FMV*
			D	$80	$500
			E	80	500
			F	80	500
				$240	$1500

Assume that the equipment was purchased by the partnership for $400, and that the land is used in the partnership's business.

Questions:

1. Before the distribution to B in liquidation of her interest in the partnership, what is her outside basis?

2. If there were a § 754 election in place what would be the amount of the § 743(b) adjustment, and among which assets (and in what amounts) would it be allocated?

3. What are the income tax consequences to B of the $500 distribution?

4. What difference would it have made if the agreement explicitly allocated $100 to goodwill?

5. What difference would it have made if there were no buy/sell agreement and B (who is also a doctor) becomes a partner in D's place?

Chapter Fifteen
Disguised Sales and Exchanges

A. Disguised Sales of Property

Assignment:

Logic: Chapter Fifteen, pp. 218-34

Code: §§ 704(c)(1)(B), 737, 707(a)(2)(B).

Regulations: §§ 1.707-3(a) through (e), (f) Ex. 1, 2, 3 and 8; 1.707-5(a) through (e), (f) Ex. 1, 2, 4, 5, 6, 8 and 10; -6(a), (b)(1), (b)(2)(iii), (d); -8; 1.737-1. Skim § 1.707-4.

Recommended Reading: Otey v. Commissioner, 634 F.2d 1046 (6th Cir. 1980)

Problems:

1. A, B and C form the ABC partnership. A contributes land worth $2500 in which A has a basis of $1000. B and C each contributes $1000 cash.. A is to have a 50% interest in profits, losses, and capital; B and C are each to have 25% interests. As part of the basic business transaction, shortly after formation, the partnership distributes $500 to A. What are the tax consequences to A and the partnership as a result of this transaction?

   (i) How would your analysis change if the distribution to equalize capital accounts occurred one year after formation? Three years after formation? Numbers are not necessary.

   (ii) Suppose, instead of distributing $500 cash, the partnership purchased a bond for $500. According to the partnership agreement, A is allocated 99% of all income, gain and loss from the bond. All other partnership items are allocated 50-25-25. Three years after formation, the bond is distributed to A.

2. Assume the same facts in #1, except that the property is worth $4000 and is subject to a $2000 recourse mortgage, and there is no distribution planned.   Assume, in the alternative,

   (i)   The mortgage was incurred five years ago to finance another investment;
   (ii)   The mortgage was incurred last year to acquire the property;
   (iii)   The mortgage was incurred last year to make capital improvements on the property;
   (iv)   The mortgage was incurred three days before the partnership was formed; the proceeds were used to acquire stock.

3. How would your answer change to 2(iv) change if the mortgage were nonrecourse?

4. How would your answer change to 2 (i) if the property were worth $4500 and A received $500 cash distribution from the partnership at the time of contribution?

5. On January 1, 2005, X, Y, and Z form an equal partnership to which X contributes Blackacre (value = $1000, basis = $600), Y contributes nonmarketable securities (value = $1000, basis = $200), and Z contributed $1000 cash. The partnership uses the cash to buy Greenacre. All three assets are capital assets in the partnership's hands. On January 1, 2008, the partnership's balance sheet is as follows:

Asset	Basis	Book	FMV
Blackacre	$600	$1000	$1500
Greenacre	1000	1000	1500
Securities	200	1000	1500

		Capital Accounts	
		Tax	Book
	X	$600	$1000
	Y	200	1000
	Z	1000	1000

On this date, the following alternative distributions take place. What are the tax consequences to all parties of each of distribution?

a. Z receives Blackacre in complete liquidation of her interest in the partnership. How would your answer change, if at all, if Blackacre were worth only $800 on the date of distribution?

b. Y receives Greenacre in complete liquidation of her interest in the partnership.

c. Y receives Blackacre in complete distribution of her interest in the partnership.

B. Disguised Sales of Partnership Interests

Assignment:

Logic:
Chapter Fifteen, pp.234-236

Code: §§ 721, 722, 723, 707(a)(2)(B), 731(a), 732(a) & (b). Generally review §§
                1001; 453(a), (b) & (c); 453A(a) & (b); 1012; 1274

Prop. Regs: §§ 1.707-7(a) – (l), [Omit examples (4) & (5)]

Questions:

1. A, B and C are equal partners in PRS, a general partnership, which has the following
assets and no liabilities:

	AB/Book	*FMV*
Cash	$800	$800
Blackacre	800	1000
Whiteacre	600	1500
Greenacre	800	1200
	$3000	$4500

Blackacre, Whiteacre and Greenacre are capital assets held by PRS as investments. A, B
and C each has a basis in her partnership interest of $1000.

In (a)-(d), all transfers occur on February 7, 2007.

(a) X contributes $750 to PRS in exchange for a 1/6 interest in the partnership, and PRS
distributes $750 of cash to A, reducing A's interest in the partnership from 1/3 to 1/6. If
these two events are respected as independent events, what are the tax consequences to
each of the parties?

(b) Under the proposed regulations, how would these transactions be treated for tax
purposes?

(c) X contributes $1500 cash for an interest in PRS and PRS distributes Whiteacre to A
in complete liquidation of her interest in PRS. What are the tax consequences to A, X
and PRS?

(d) X contributes $750 for an interest in PRS and PRS Whiteacre to A in complete
liquidation of her interest in PRS. What are the tax consequences to A, X and PRS?

(e) What difference would it make in (c) if X contributed $1500 to PRS on February 1, 2007, and PRS distributed Whiteacre to A on March 1, 2008? On March 1, 2009?

(f) What difference would it make in (c) if PRS distributed Whiteacre to A on February 1, 2007 and X contributed $1500 cash on March 1, 2008?

(g) What difference would it make in (c) if on February 1, 2007 X contributed $1500 cash and one month later PRS distributed $1500 to A in liquidation of her interest?

2. X and Y are equal partners in PRS, a general partnership, and each partner has an outside basis of $700. On January 1, 2007, PRS has the following assets and liabilities:

	AB/Book	*FMV*	
Cash	$200	$200	Mortgage $400
Blackacre	800	1200	
Whiteacre	400	1400	
	$1400	$2800	

On this date, Z contributes $600 cash to PRS for a 25% interest in the partnership, and PRS distributes $600 cash to X, reducing X's interest in PRS to 25%. The mortgage is fully recourse and is shared among the partners in proportion to their interests in PRS. What are the tax consequences as a result of these transactions?